D0629914

Catfulness

Catfulness

PAOLO VALENTINO

TRANSLATED FROM THE ITALIAN BY
CHENXIN JIANG

Quercus

First published in Great Britain in 2017 by
Quercus Editions Ltd
Carmelite House
50 Victoria Embankment
London EC4Y 0DZ
An Hachette UK company

A CIP catalogue record for this book is available
from the British Library

ISBN 978 1 63506 150 5

10 9 8 7 6 5 4 3

Printed and bound in China

A cat's guide to achieving mindfulness

Introduction

'I've lived with many Zen masters – they were all cats.' 'I think cats are spirits come to earth. I'm convinced they can walk on clouds.' 'There's nothing sweeter than the sense of peace that comes over a cat when it's resting, and nothing livelier than a cat in motion . . .' I could go on, because human beings have said just about everything there is to say about us cats.

As a cat myself, I don't know how much of it is true. When it comes down to it, I'm just living my life. I don't go troubling myself with what might have happened during my previous lives or what could happen in a future one. The future is a projection of the mind: why worry about it right now?

But I can understand why human beings have thought of us, since time immemorial, as little monks in meditation. Sometimes they've even taken us to be gods – which, of course, we'd gladly have them believe.

Human beings are capable of creating, all by themselves, an entire world of problems.

I see that, as all cats do. Humans can't stay still for a moment, and one of their greatest tasks is to find more tasks to take on, as if they can't let themselves take a break even for a minute. They often fail to express what's inside them – they might want one thing, but they'll claim they want something else if they're worried about hurting someone's feelings. Some of them raise their voices as if to talk over the other person, while others move nervously, pacing back and forth across a room, shaking their arms and legs, bobbing their heads ... They're always pursuing something else, as if the life they're already living isn't enough. They call it the pursuit of 'happiness', but do they even know what happiness is?

Luckily, they've got us cats.

We eat when we're hungry, drink when we're thirsty and sleep when we're sleepy. We live only in the present, one moment at a time. We don't have to worry about pleasing other cats – so instead, we can live in a way that makes our innermost selves happy.

It's a little like *mindfulness*; the art of living in the present moment. After all, we cats have always practised it.

If human beings could learn to observe us cats more closely, the world we live in would definitely be a calmer one. All it would take is for them to stop and spend time with us a little more often, to stroke us, play with us, brush our fur, without thinking about how they're supposed to be working on some task or other. Because the most important task is to be happy.

Or as Sigmund Freud put it: 'Time spent with a cat is never time wasted.'

In this book, I wanted to put down everything human beings can do to be happy finally. It is a seven-week programme, and putting these instructions into practice will allow you to begin a form of existence that's free from the burdens and constraints that anchor human souls to earth.

Who knows if a new life will start for you . . .

FIRST
WEEK

Stop and relax

If you spend your whole life thinking and doing things,
doing things and thinking, it's as if you never lived.
Why don't you stop, relax,
and pay attention to what's going on inside you instead?
You'll find that the world goes on
without you, without your anxieties
and worries: just watch
and keep a distance, the way I do,
looking down from the highest shelf in the living room.
In that moment, you'll have truly lived.

13

Everything can be a game

The game is to keep experimenting,
to test out your five senses and keep
discovering new things about yourself and the world.
Don't grow complacent with your usual
comforting pastimes: find some new ones
or turn your habits into a game.
You're not being silly: rather, it's silly
to think growing up means you have to stop playing games!

Be patient

I can wait motionless in front
of a mouse hole for hours.
Neither wall clocks nor
internal clocks exist for me
when something so important is at stake.
It's no coincidence that a Sufi master,
when asked: 'From whom did you learn to meditate?'
responded: 'From a cat lurking in front of a mouse hole.'

15

Don't turn off your curiosity

What's behind that piece of furniture?
What can you discover by climbing to the
    highest point in the house?
What could be hiding behind a closed gate
or at the end of a street you've never gone down?
Don't turn off your curiosity
and life will continue to deliver,
day by day, big and small surprises.

Gaze at an aquarium

If you want to deal with stress, gaze at an aquarium.
It doesn't matter how big it is.
All that matters is that there are fish inside
– from ordinary goldfish
to colourful tropical fish –
fish swimming: their gentle,
almost hypnotic movements and slow breathing
dispel all ugly thoughts.

Immerse yourself in the outdoors

When the hustle and bustle is getting the best of you,
  just turn it off.
Go outside – go onto the balcony, care for the plants,
or go for a walk in the park if you can.
Hurl yourself into a field without thinking about it.
There, in the great outdoors, where life
is in harmony with the ancestral rhythms of nature,
where the grass grows on its own
without needing your help,
you'll rediscover peace in a moment.

Day of rest

Today is Sunday, so rest.
Erase the word 'task' from this day
and let your mind empty itself . . .
Above all, don't think about the fact
that tomorrow will be Monday again.
Tomorrow is tomorrow,
and the present is the present.

19

Rediscover the world

Don't ever take your surroundings for granted. Curiosity is a form of therapy that you shouldn't forget to practise on a daily basis. When curiosity is suspended, you can get bored and frustrated. You might even begin to feel the desire to escape.

The world can always be full of surprises if you learn to look at it the right way: nothing, fundamentally, is ever exactly as you expect. Every day can be an occasion for rediscovering the world around you, observing it attentively with all five of your senses. Any object can be a new discovery.

Take an everyday object you've had for years: an ornament you bought on holiday, for instance. Hold it in your hands, take a close look at it, smell it, and ask yourself how it's made, how many people put work and effort into it. You'll grow to appreciate the object even more.

When you're dusting the shelves, take all the books off, and glance at their covers as you put them back. Have you read them all? When did you read them? What emotions did they inspire? Why don't you try cracking open one of the ones you haven't read?

Observe day by day, or even over the course of a single day, how the potted plants on your balcony change, or the plants in your garden. Isn't there so much life, even inside a silent plant?

SECOND
WEEK

Shake off those accessories

There's only one way to feel free:
drop all the burdens you have.
Even accessories can be a burden.
I prefer not to wear a ribbon, bells, clothes.
If you sense a burden
  – regardless of whether it's a small thing
   or something unbearable –
just do the simplest thing: let it fall.

25

Enjoy your daily routine

Your everyday life isn't
a cage you have to escape.
The cumulative pleasure of every little action
can lead to happiness: waking up,
eating out of the bowl, falling asleep,
waking up again, running, jumping . . .
That's what the Bodhidharma said:
Zen is neither more nor less than everyday life.

Don't fall for the frenzy

Someone with a full calendar
who's always travelling and taking part in thousands
    of worldly events
can be fascinating – I know.
And, by contrast, your life,
which perhaps isn't quite so exciting,
may feel rather boring.
But the truth is that frenetic living
isn't that interesting after all: I have very little to do,
doing the same things over and over again,
    and I live well this way.

What's right and what's wrong?

In life there are no such things as right or wrong,
they're nothing more than a 'donkey's bit and collar'.
That's what an ancient Zen saying tells us.
Don't do everything the usual, 'right' way.
I, for one, am always experimenting with new ways
of reaching the windowsill:
I climb on things, walk across the desk,
jump, and sometimes fall.
Allow yourself to 'fail':
you'll enjoy the results.

Essential grooming

Combing your hair or allowing it to be combed
by a loved one isn't just
a moment of pleasure you're giving
    yourself.
Combing your hair
slowly and repeatedly,
it turns out, stimulates many of the shiatsu
pressure points that produce pleasure.
But please don't forget
to comb my fur too: that's
our special moment of intimacy!

29

If you want something, speak up

Silence can be your worst enemy.
If you really want something,
even if you risk hurting
someone else's feelings,
speak up loudly
and make your feelings heard.
Otherwise, everything you didn't say
will stay within you and slowly eat away at you
    from the inside.

Day of rest

It's said that not doing anything
is the most difficult thing in the world.
Maybe it's that way for human beings,
who still have very, very much
to learn on the subject,
but not necessarily for cats.
So this is
the only 'task' you're going to
    give yourself today.

Cultivate a ritual

We cats are animals of habit. We like doing more or less the same things every day, with a little variation every now and then, just so things don't get too boring. This is because we love our lives, we love what we do, and we're not dreaming of living completely different lives, as human beings so often are.

This exercise aims to help you better appreciate what you have too.

 Choose a daily habit that feels like a chore, like brushing your teeth in the morning or putting the rubbish out.

 Try telling yourself: 'Ah, how wonderful it is to be doing this right now!' It might feel ridiculous at first, but trust me – just do it.

The next time you do this task, don't think about what you're going to do as soon as you're done with it, think with your whole self about what you're doing right now. For instance, if you're brushing your teeth, concentrate on the sensation of the toothbrush against your teeth, the taste of the toothpaste melting onto your tongue, your palate. In that moment, you are *simply* brushing your teeth.

Repeat this for a week. I'm sure on the seventh day of brushing your teeth or taking the rubbish out, it will no longer be merely a chore you have to get through in order to move on to something more interesting or useful.

THIRD
WEEK

Break your habits

There's nothing stopping you from changing
your habits,
not even your desires.
Why do you always sleep in the same bed
when there are plenty of other places in the house
where you could take a nap?
That will help you avoid making habits

and find that the only secure and immovable place
is within you – no matter where you are.

Get up and keep walking

You can fall, you can hurt yourself,
you can be disappointed,
but then you have to get up.
After first one fall and then another,
you'll learn to avoid
the blows, to recognize danger from a distance,
but you also won't be disheartened,
you'll be able to cope with setbacks.
I have nine lives, and every time I'm reborn
I'm even happier than I was before.

Enjoy the view

Carve out some time every day
to stand at the windowsill and admire the view.
Watch life go on outside your home:
cars passing, people walking,
birds flying . . . and then concentrate
on the furthest point of the horizon.
Your eyes will relax and you'll feel
a new space, all yours,
being created inside you.

39

Let it out: it's normal

Don't think that letting it out every now and then,
or whenever you feel you need to,
makes you a worse person.
Every living thing has two souls:
a tranquil soul and a restless one.
So don't ask yourself why
I sometimes spring to my feet for no reason.
Rather, let your 'darker'
side come out if it wants:
that's the only way to stop it from
   devouring you.

Fear will pass

Emotions expire after some time:
just as quickly as they appeared to illuminate
or cloud the mind, they leave.
The same goes for fear, the emotion
that keeps us away from danger.
When the emergency is over, however,
don't keep dwelling on the
danger you escaped and everything you risked:
free your mind to make room
for new and better emotions.

Learn to say no

'The scalded cat is afraid of cold water.'
That's what they say, and it's true.
Remember what's hurt you before
and don't allow it to hurt you
again: you don't actually have to
do what other people want.

Learn to say no: the first time it will be a surprise,
and then it will be your best weapon for leading a
  more tranquil life.

Day of rest

Idleness is the father of all philosophy.
So said a famous philosopher.
Perhaps he only meant that
when you stop struggling with
obsessive thoughts,
a crystal clear
true way of thinking
can finally come to light?

43

Don't be trapped by the everyday

Life isn't always special or extraordinary: it's made up of habits, actions that have to be repeated day after day.

But there's a difference between a daily existence lived mindfully, in which you appreciate every single one of your own movements, and an existence lived on autopilot, without paying attention to what you're doing – or worse still, a tense existence that feels as if you're trapped in a prison that can't be escaped.

When escape seems like the only way out, it's a sign that you're not living in the present and that you have to do something to start appreciating everyday life again. One way of doing this might be to tweak some of your own habits.

 Try figuring out whether at home, or in the restaurant where you spend your lunch break, you always sit in the same seat. Now switch to a

----

different one; suddenly the same old world, seen from a new perspective, will seem new to you. Nothing will really have changed. You'll just have stopped taking your surroundings for granted.

If you always take the same street to work, try walking along a different one. It might take you a few more minutes, but you'll be starting the day in an unusual way.

Go for a walk in your neighbourhood even if you don't have anywhere to go or any errands to run. Simply put one foot in front of another and look around, sharpen your sense of smell, listen to passers-by talk and cars whoosh by. You'll truly feel part of life itself.

FOURTH
WEEK

Don't always be looking elsewhere

Don't believe that wonder
and discovery are necessarily far away, elsewhere.
I only dream of passing my life
in the places I already know:
my couch, the windowsill, the mat I scratch at.
The real journey, an author once wrote,
does not consist in seeking out new places,
but in having new eyes.

49

Be yours and yours only

Don't let other people treat you as
their property, or worse,
as their conquest.
Inside you, there is
a pure, deep something
that no one else can
take away or subjugate.
Preserve it, even at the cost of
seeming aloof: that's you, and
losing it means losing your happiness.

A change of perspective

Why do I prefer a cardboard box
to the soft cushion you just bought me?
Why don't you ask yourself:
why does the creaky bed
in a mountain cabin feel cosier
than a comfy hotel bed?
It's all a matter of perspective.
Be honest with yourself, and don't choose
the option that's supposedly better,
but the one that makes you happier.

It's a matter of poise

Spend some time watching an animal that wags its tail
at any old thing,
and think about how much energy it's wasting.
Sometimes it's better to maintain a healthy degree of poise:
gesticulate less,
speak in a softer voice,
breathe and speak more slowly . . .
There's no need to always be
over the top
in order to get noticed by other people.

Keep your home clean

Your home is your little realm,
the place where you can feel tranquil,
satisfied and serene.
So keep it clean and
keep your things in order,
so that its order and cleanliness
can become
an interior order and cleanliness,
which will allow you to see
each one of your emotions more clearly.

53

Tenderness is a form of strength

A severe expression,
distant demeanour
or hard words will not make you stronger,
endear you to others or win you respect.
On the contrary, don't ever be afraid
of showing your affectionate side and admitting
you need a cuddle.
In return, you'll receive
all the love you deserve.

54

Day of rest

It's Sunday again.
Take advantage of this day and be idle.
When you are completely at rest,
just as when you're dreaming,
the submerged truth will come to the surface.
That's what a great author once said.
I say – and perhaps it's the same thing –
that idleness helps your
interior self re-emerge.

55

Make an effort to stay calm

Have you ever tried watching a nervous person? Watch how they fidget with their hands, tap their feet or raise their voices suddenly. Is there anything more annoying than that? It's no coincidence that we cats prefer calm, quiet people with whom we can share a moment of deep tranquillity.

Even though sometimes our meowing can be irritating (though it's only to make ourselves heard when absolutely necessary!), our purring, with its low, pleasing sound, can perhaps spur you to aim for a self-confidence that inspires respect.

To begin with, though, learn to observe yourself: are you a nervous person too? Do you, for instance, raise your voice or make sudden movements? If so, you can start saying to yourself right now: 'Be calm', and try a few small experiments.

When you're in the middle of an argument and feel attacked, instead of lashing out, think of the Sphinx surrounded by sand dunes, unmoving, guarding the pyramids with her feline body. Then breathe deeply and make an effort to talk back to your interlocutor in a calm tone. He or she will be taken aback and the tension might even (not that it's entirely up to you!) dissipate.

 When your partner comes home, don't overwhelm them with questions and demands right away, passing your tension on to them. Think about the fact that they've had a busy day too. Greet them gently and calmly and address them in a quiet voice. That will make your evening a relaxing one.

FIFTH WEEK

Don't give yourself too many rules

You've always been told to eat,
bathe and wake up
at a regular time.
Your day is determined
by a tight, precise schedule.
Instead, I'm telling you:
eat when you want to,
bathe when you feel the need,
wake up when your eyes
open of their own accord.
That's what Zen is.

61

62

Allow yourself to nap

Idleness is an art.
In a world that races along
and hardly ever gives itself a break,
rediscover the joy of a yawn
and a short afternoon break.
Give your body over to slumber
and close your eyes. It won't be wasted time:
when you get up, you'll have all the energy
    you need
to go about your day better.
My motto is: 'Sleep and let sleep.'

Be grateful

Don't think about it: if you're happy, be grateful.
I show my gratitude by purring
or leaving a special present at the foot of your bed,
a sparrow or a little bird
I caught just for you.
You can show gratitude with a smile or a gentle word
for whoever's made your day a better one.
And every morning, when you get up,
be grateful to life:
the following day, you'll have even more
to be thankful for.

63

Don't ever give up

What is a prohibition? It's just something in the mind that
prevents us from imagining other ways of living
and realizing our dreams.
Prohibitions don't exist for me:
I only give up
when I lose interest in something.
If I want it, I can be very,
very stubborn. Which is also to be
very, very honest
with yourself, and hence to be more serene.

Be friends with emptiness

Don't be afraid of emptiness:
every now and then, liberate your mind completely
from its thoughts and burdens.
Let go and spend all the time you like
with your eyes closed, in emptiness.
A little like me.
Emptiness is not a shortcoming.
On the contrary, I maintain
 – even though I don't expect you
    to understand right away –
that emptiness and abundance are the same thing.

65

Defend your territory

It's not necessary to go off and conquer the world
when you're already the unchallenged king of your own
    territory.
No matter how small it is, it's your realm, your home:
make it like yourself, make it in your own image,
in harmony in every way with your habits,
and don't ever allow anyone to
invade it.

Day of rest

No living creature is free
if it can't be idle every now and again.
If you want to feel truly free,
independent, just as self-satisfied as a cat,
choose to forgo work today.
Don't allow yourself to believe that
only 'useful' things can be good for you.

67

Be appreciative

There's so much in the world to be grateful for: a cat bowl filled daily, fresh water to sip on when you feel like it, a walk through the potted plants on the balcony, a clean and orderly house, an affectionate caress, a reward that makes the day even more special. You human beings often express your emotions only when they are negative: anger, resentment, sadness . . . as if expressing positive emotions would make you feel guilty.

It's time to notice when you're happy. That alone will make you exponentially happier.

 Choose a moment of the day in which you're calm and relaxed: it could be a lunch break in a sunny park just a stone's throw from your office, or that moment in bed when sleepiness is beginning to make your eyelids grow heavy.

Take a pen and paper and write down everything good that's happened to you during the day, everything you're grateful for. If nothing special has happened – like an unexpected gift, a promotion, or a friendly encounter – think about your everyday life: your family, the people you had dinner with . . . the cat who purrs at you when you come home.

 Reread the list and be mentally grateful for every single thing that has happened to you.

Repeat the exercise one to three times per week. The more you do it, the happier and more grateful to life you'll be.

SIXTH
WEEK

Love yourself

There's no one in the world
who's more important than you.
Don't ever forget who you are,
consider your own needs and your happiness
ahead of everything else: soon you'll realize
that this isn't an act of selfishness on your part
even if someone might try to tell you so.
Don't pay them any mind: if you're happier,
you'll infect the people around you
with the happiness inside you.

Breathe with your stomach

Watch my stomach while I'm sleeping,
see how it rises and falls.
Don't you feel calmer
just looking at me?
That's an abdominal breath,
the deepest kind of breathing.

Only by making an effort to breathe this way
can you fill your whole body with oxygen,
relax your diaphragm,
keep anxiety at bay, and even
fall asleep more easily.

Wake up at dawn

Sometimes you wake up early,
not long before the sun rises,
while the others are still sleeping,
and witness the everyday miracle of dawn.
That's the most precious moment
of the whole day, the moment
in which the world is flooded with light
and everything seems to be reborn.

75

Enjoy every one of your meals

Be grateful to the hand
that puts food on your table.
And enjoy your food with relish.
It doesn't matter whether
you have something different to eat every day:
indeed, why change things so much?
Appreciate what you have, enjoy it thoroughly,
and when you receive something unusual
it'll make you a hundred times happier.

Be independent

Being independent the way I am
doesn't mean having to reject others
or never asking anyone for help
(on the contrary, if you need help you should say so!).
It means being able to enjoy life
even when you're alone, learning to satisfy
your own needs, and not being
emotionally dependent on
other people's approval.

Take care of your body

Don't treat the need to take care of yourself as a chore:
practise it as an act of love
towards yourself, something just for you, turn
cleaning the house into a pleasant, reassuring ritual.
We cats spend almost
ten per cent of our day on hygiene:
if your body is happy, your mind is too.

Day of rest

Just today, at least, don't set an alarm clock.
If you wake up early anyway,
enjoy the first light of the day
and linger in bed doing nothing for a little longer.
Someone once said that the happiest part
of a person's day are the moments
they spend awake in bed in the mornings.

19

Relearn how to breathe

Human beings have forgotten how to breathe. Most of you only breathe with your chest, especially when you're stressed out. This eventually causes tension in your diaphragm, neck and back …There's nothing better for your body and healthier for your mind than breathing deeply through the stomach. Becoming aware of your breath means you've become more aware of yourself, your emotions and your energy.

 Lie down in a comfortable position. You can choose your bed, a mattress, or a carpet. Extend your legs, or if you prefer, bend them with your feet on the floor. Abdominal breathing can also be done if you're sitting with your back straight, or even standing. Really, do it however you like: the important thing is to breathe.

Put one hand on your belly button without exerting any pressure on it, and then breathe in deeply and feel your stomach expand like a balloon. You'll feel your hand rise as it rests on your abdomen.

 Breathe out and feel your hand fall along with your abdomen as it contracts. If you like, you can try exhaling even more deeply, completely emptying your stomach to allow for even deeper circulation of air.

 Begin to inhale and exhale evenly, and then try to increase the length of time in which you exhale until you reach a 2:1 ratio. For instance, you might breathe in for five seconds and breathe out for ten seconds.

SEVENTH
WEEK

Don't think too hard, act

If you try to figure everything out in your mind
you'll just end up getting even more muddled.
Sometimes, the best way to
cope with your life
is to allow your body and instincts
to be your guide.
And if this leads to a fall,
think nothing of it: in a moment
you'll have forgotten all about it.

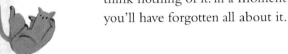

85

The art of stretching

The body mirrors the interior world.
And that is where all the tension
of the day accumulates.
Get into good habits:
stretch out every now and again on a bed
or, even better, a carpet,
and enjoy the pleasing and liberating
sensations within you.
You'll feel less tense right away.

Ignore people who irritate you

To stay calm, keep a distance
from people who are too loud or too nervous.
They aren't the best company
for someone who loves silence . . .
and a little snuggling.
Above all, if someone is irritating
or provoking you, take the easiest path: ignore them!
You might come across as arrogant
but you'll save yourself a lot of unnecessary stress.

87

Sharpen your sense of smell

You have five senses, all of which
give you enjoyable sensations.
Don't fall into the trap of thinking about smell
only when you sniff something putrid.
Sharpen your sense of smell
by looking for fragrant, pleasing aromas
that relax you and remind you
how extraordinary the world you live in
can sometimes be.

Eat when you feel like it

Why force yourself to finish
everything on your plate
even when you don't feel like it?
As soon as you feel full
it's better to stop eating.
Learn to listen to your body:
it'll tell you when it's time to eat
and whether you need a little snack
or a full meal.

Choose sun

The sun is a bath of energy
that is completely available to us.
When its rays penetrate the clouds,
let the sunlight bathe your face and warm your skin.
Feel your body relax, feel yourself calm down.

90

Surrender completely to the heat:
stretch, spin around and think about
what a wonderful and simple gift you're giving yourself.

Day of rest

Human beings don't know
how to just stay in one room.
This explains all their problems,
as a great thinker pointed out centuries ago.
Let your Sunday be like every day for me:
a time to discover the
pure joy of being alive in the world.
Without anything to do.

91

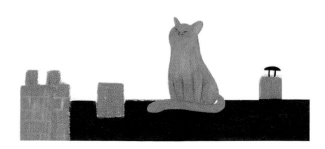

Feline stretching

Exercise doesn't necessarily have to involve competing against yourself and other people. You don't have to be looking in the mirror after a workout and telling yourself: yes, I'm strong!

Think of it this way: exercise can be an opportunity to expel all the tension your body has accumulated over the course of a day, particularly the tension in your back.

Feline stretching does precisely that. When you're practising it, think about me, and how I arch my back and stretch, raising my head to the ceiling. That will make it easier for you!

 Get down on your hands and knees on a comfortable surface. If possible, put a cushion beneath your knees to protect them. Your thighs and arms should be perpendicular to the ground, your knees should be in line with your hips, and your wrists should be directly below your elbows.

Exhale. Gently arch your back while lowering your head towards the ground.

Inhale. Gently lower your back until it is no longer arched. While you're doing so, lift your head high.

Repeat this motion, focusing on making your breathing more relaxed and your movement more expansive.

For Nigel, Panda-Thérèse, Shiro, Olivia, Pigna, Cavour, Emilio, Tina, Romeo, Stregatto, Camillo, Mimì, la Maffy, Vladimiro, Trombino, Peppe, Magneto, Mizzi, Ampelio, Cat, Rouge, Lizzie, Beirut, Isi, Zanzibar, Cheope, Malachia, Trudy, Nausicaa, Asia, Ginger, Pepe, Camilla, Beatrice, Filini, Prika, Pigne, Batuffolo, Cremino, Jack, Minù, Swift, Rufo, Spritz, Libano, Enough, Already, Rosso, Fiocco, Kamala, Melo, Maya, Giotto, Dafne, Chicco, Ginevra, Linda, Tigro, Saphir and all the other cats in the world who make their human friends happy.